DO WHAT
YOU DO

THE **SECOND** EDITION

OUTSOURCING AS CAPACITY BUILDING
IN THE NONPROFIT SECTOR

JEFF RUSSELL

Published by Elevate. An imprint of Elevate Publishing, Boise, ID.

Web: http://www.elevatepub.com

This book may be purchased in bulk for educational, business, non-profit or promotional use.

For information please email info@elevatepub.com.

ISBN (print): 9781943425938
ISBN (e-book): 9781943425945

Library of Congress Control Number: 2016942585

Printed in the United States of America

DEDICATION

This book is dedicated to my beautiful wife, Tara, who has supported me through the entrepreneurial years of Jitasa. I could not have done any of this without her steadfast support and grace.

And to our children, Tyson and Lucy, who have made the journey so much more enjoyable, lively, and fun.

Lastly, this book is for all of those in the world, especially Executive Directors, who work tirelessly and often unrecognized, to make the world a better, smarter, more beautiful place.

TABLE OF CONTENTS

FOREWORD

It's an increasingly familiar story for many attracted to the mission-driven world of nonprofit and non-governmental organizations. "I joined this organization to save/protect/improve/stand up for [fill in the blank with some admirable goals] and what I ended up doing was boring business stuff I hate and am no good at." Sure enough, at some point in a nonprofit's existence, especially if it grows large and the leaders become more senior, running the organization seems to take more time than pursuing the admirable goals that define one's reason for being there. Burn-out, turn-over, and succession crises highlight the human consequences. Lagging revenues, auditing and control discrepancies, and problems with the IRS signal financial ones. Missed program targets, unserved and dissatisfied clients, and unhappy boards of directors sound warnings even more dire.

"Capacity building" is the usual prescription to set matters straight, and this usually means training in the human resources, financial, and business-management skills that seem to be lacking. The prescription itself is often bitter—something akin to "Eat your spinach, it's good for you" for the goals-motivated nonprofit leader who would much prefer a more satisfying, albeit metaphorical, cheeseburger and Coke.

Other problems arise. Train the staff in various technical skills and they may leave for better paying jobs elsewhere. They may also leave for jobs where they don't need to be technically challenged, but where the mission and goals are more compelling and occupy more of the working day. Many nonprofits are small in size, which means pulling a critical staff member "off the line" to take a business or management course could very well cripple the operation, if not permanently then at least for the time spent away. Non-profit boards often have business leaders on them who are usually there to share their own wealth and to provide access to other donors. In times of organizational stress and challenge, the knee-jerk reaction to "run this place like a real business" can be substantial, even overwhelming. It may also only make matters worse in terms of employee morale, energy and dedication—the very resources upon which any successful nonprofit is founded and depends.

As the sheer number of nonprofit organizations continues to grow, these kinds of problems and many other related ones also grow. Indeed, the increasing number itself is thought to be a problem best solved by "mergers and acquisitions" so as to attain what economics textbooks call economies of scale. Why, for example, should it be that there are nearly 300 different nonprofit environment and conservation organizations operating in the Greater Yellowstone Ecosystem? "Obviously" the need to consolidate and streamline will make for a much smaller number of more efficient and effective operations.

Actually, the conventional wisdom of "obvious" measures and means—bitter pills and spinach—to improve nonprofit performance is flawed. It comes up short in case after case. Even worse, when applied it can actually make matters worse.

Jeff Russell, in this wonderfully wise and insightful book, sums matters up: *Do What You Do Best: Outsourcing as Capacity Build-*

ing in the Nonprofit Sector. The following sharp observations sketch some of the basics.

"Small can be beautiful," and there may even be an optimal—small—size for nonprofits where they can maintain sharp focus on a mission and goals.

"Economies of scale" can at the same time be achieved by outsourcing non-core functions of many separate organizations and thus freeing up time and energy to pursue the one or two things where each excels.

"Control" over processes and personnel can be enhanced by outsourcing business and technical functions rather than "Doing It Yourself."

"Processes" within the organization can be standardized and streamlined as one interacts routinely with an outsourcing partner. The relationship is on-going and co-dependent which makes for continuous learning and improvement.

"Not knowing" a technical tool or business skill in some detail is not the same as "Knowing How to Use" a tool or skill. Understanding what a financial statement actually means is far more important than being able to generate the statement in the first place.

Jeff, his wife Tara, and his colleagues at Jitasa (originally named Easy Office here at Yale) put to very practical uses these and many other insights and lessons. Indeed, the book shares many personal experiences and decisions that led up to the creation of Jitasa. There is a forthright commitment to the nonprofit sector that makes their organization, and this book, stand out and shine brightly. It's almost no wonder, even though it's a bit ironic, that one of their biggest "partners" is the Boy Scouts of America. Just the choice of the label *partner* in preference to client or other usual terms tells you something about their approach.

But do not be misled by the open and earnest style. Russell and his organization are exceptionally experienced and skilled. Jeff is a Georgia Tech engineer who spent his first ten years at consultant heavy-weight Accenture helping dozens of Fortune 500 companies outsource mainly to make more money. At some point while working on a Nike project in Bangkok he realized that as important as profit is, there were other things that mattered as well. His turn to social causes and missions came then, and so he headed off to Yale's School of Management for his MBA.

The School has a reputation in nonprofit management and in social enterprises, and Jeff took advantage. His prize-winning business strategy plan was the plan for Jitasa. Along the way Jeff participated in the weekly "Organization Effectiveness" workshop and seminar, a place where experiences, works in progress, research, and outside visitors from the nonprofit world routinely come together. One summer he worked with me to help with an ambitious survey and stock-taking, previously noted, of all the nonprofit organizations in the Greater Yellowstone Ecosystem. Not only were we surprised by the large number, but we both learned some valuable lessons about personalities, egos, denial, and reluctance to yield control.

If there are simple messages—or "Take Homes" in B-School Speak—that summarize Jeff, his organization, and this book, it might be to focus sharply, relentlessly, and from the heart in a never-ending search to *Do What You Do Best.*

Garry D. Brewer
Yale School of Management

INTRODUCTION

*No man is an island entire of itself; every man
is a piece of the continent, a part of the main.*
—John Donne, poet

From an early age, we all learn to do what we do best. Life naturally rewards us for the things we do well. I saw this in action as I watched my children learn to walk. They learned that walking barefoot on the carpet was easier than walking on the hardwood floor with socks. After they bounced their heads on the hardwood a few times, they learned this wasn't something they did all that well. They retreated to the carpet, honed their skills, and soon were ready for the hardwood. We are naturally built to avoid negative consequences and to focus on activities where we succeed.

As we get older, we begin to see interdependence in society and learn the value of teamwork. In kindergarten we learn that when we go out into the big, bad world we have to hold hands and stick together. We are better together than apart. As we moved into childhood activities and sports, this concept of integration and teamwork continued to be enforced. In a good choir some people sing bass and some sing soprano. A good band has some people who rock the violin and some who play the flute. Each person is doing what he or she does best, and the orchestra is better because of this specialization. A good football team has huge, heavy linemen and smaller, quicker running backs. Each person does what he does best.

These same concepts of teamwork and interdependence that applied to us in kindergarten still apply to each of us today. And they apply to our organizations and our society: we are not islands; we are all "part of the main." When all members do their respective parts and do what they do best, all prosper.

There are over one million nonprofits in America today. It is a vast ecosystem of people working together to make the world a better place. Nonprofits fill a niche in our interconnected society. Business, government, places of worship, and our education system all have needed and necessary roles in society. We can all argue—and often do—about their relative value and how big their roles should be, but I don't think anyone would argue that they have no role. It is the same within nonprofits and within the "social sector." We all have a role to play and each organization plays a different role.

MY JOURNEY

During my undergraduate studies I struggled with what my role in society should be. Like most engineering students at Georgia Tech, I spent six months a year in class and six months a year working as a co-op, which is a recurring internship. For my co-op position, I worked with Accenture, a Fortune 500 consulting firm with 65,000 employees around the globe. I was pretty low on the organizational chart, but I got fantastic exposure to the world of big business. By being a note-taker for senior Accenture executives, I got to watch from inside the room how decisions were made. The experience, I have to admit, was intoxicating. I traveled America, staying in plush five-star hotels and sleeping on down pillows. To this day, I have a picture from my first business trip; I still couldn't quite imagine myself—a guy who grew up in the Mississippi countryside, cleaning out horse stalls from time to time—staying in a five-star hotel in Philadelphia. And literally fifteen days after checking out of a five-star hotel in the summer of 1996, I found myself sleeping on dirt floors in the highlands of Papua New Guinea.

In the summer of 1996, the Olympics came to Atlanta. Georgia Tech had shut down for the summer to provide its facilities to the Olympic Games and I didn't need to work at Accenture. So I spent a few months in Papua New Guinea, volunteering in the highlands outside of Goroka. I talked with former cannibals and saw people who ate the bark of trees to fill their stomachs. I met with missionaries and non-governmental organization (NGO) leaders who had dedicated their life to improving the lives of the Papua New Guineans.

The experience forced me to think about what role I wanted to play in society. Should I return to Papua New Guinea to work with indigenous people, providing them access to medical care, clean water, and healthy life habits? Or should I return to Accenture's consulting practice, five-star hotels, steakhouses, and down pillows?

My decision-making process included assessing and thinking about what I enjoyed, what I was good at doing, where I could do the most good for the most people, and what—in the quiet, still moments—I could be proud to do. Ultimately, after much introspection, I chose Corporate America as my first step.

For the next eight years I consulted for corporate giants like Nike, DuPont, Microsoft, Home Depot, and other midsize firms like Levi Strauss, Macromedia, Freightliner Trucks, and Burton Snowboards. My niche in the consulting world was outsourcing, helping organizations focus their resources on what truly helped them. We helped them focus their time, energy, and money on the tasks that helped advance their cause. And their cause was making money. Although vital and important, helping that cause grew tiresome after a while.

One day I pondered all of this as I stared out of my office window in Bangkok. I had been there for just over three years doing work for Nike, ensuring their shoeboxes were shipped around the world on time. I knew that Nike created an untold number of jobs. I had seen factories in Indonesia where 3,000 people waited at the gates outside, hoping for one day's work. Inside that factory, over 20,000 people worked creating shoes and, ultimately, providing food, shelter, and clothing for their families. They went home with the dignity of having worked, no longer dealing with the cycle of poverty that may have trapped their families for generations. I also knew that Nike minted money, and even that is not all bad.

People and conventional wisdom tend to paint shareholders as evil. However, maybe your grandmother's 401(k) or retirement fund includes Nike stock. Those returns that end up paying for her nursing home seem less evil. But I also knew that many people believed Nike made a lot of money at the expense of those poor laborers. In the '90s Nike was targeted for lax work standards and made headlines worldwide with its "sweatshops." But by the time I came around in the early 2000s, its factories were by far the cleanest and healthiest of the hundreds I toured in Asia. On top of all these things, I also knew that some kid in Des Moines wanted his new shoes to show up undamaged in a cool box. And I knew that all these things are important in our society. But for me personally, I felt a tug to connect closer to clear social causes and social impact.

As I looked out my window in Bangkok and pondered these concepts, I looked out over an urban slum community. It is a few square miles, but home to hundreds of thousands of people living in poverty, and in conditions unthinkable in America. It took me back to my time in Goroka among the rural poor. My passion and interest in being more closely connected to "doing good in the world" continued to burn in me. I could intellectually conjure up why Nike shoeboxes are good in the world, but personally, I wanted to be more closely connected. It was during this time that I decided to leave Bangkok to attend the Yale School of Management. Its slogan is "Educating Leaders for Business and Society" and its nonprofit management program is routinely ranked #1 among business schools so it seemed like a perfect fit for me. During the pursuit of my MBA, my classmates and I put together the plans that would be the foundation of Jitasa.

During this time, as I asked myself, "what do I do best?" I realized that my corporate experience had given me a depth of skills and experiences that could be used to help a broad range of socially minded organizations. My impact could be a mile wide and a few feet deep. I could help nonprofits do what they do best, by taking care of the stuff they didn't want to do. This is exactly how we had helped corporations focus. I wanted to do the same thing for nonprofits. I knew that there was an opportunity to build something that made all the benefits and virtues of shared services and outsourcing accessible to nonprofits around the country. And this journey has been the fulfillment of my personal tug-of-war to find my niche. Now, having steered Jitasa for more than five years from formation to today, I know I'm in my sweet spot. And there is no better spot to be—whether as an individual or an organization.

In *Do What You Do Best* I demonstrate how nonprofit organizations have used a variety of strategies and outsourcing concepts to further their causes. You'll learn how outsourcing has helped more Africans have clean water, helped refugees in Boise find more employment, and helped inner-city youth close the achievement gap. You will also see that doing what you do best takes great discipline. It means you may have to stop doing something you don't do as well or what distracts you from the best. Tara Russell, my wife and the CEO of Create Common Good, frequently says, "Don't let the good choke out the best." There are so many good uses of our time, but what is the best use of our time? If we spend time on activities that drain us or where we are mediocre—or even areas where we are good—we are consciously or unconsciously choosing to spend less time in areas where we are, or can be, great. Doing what you do best also means accepting help. This takes courage. King Solomon spoke to this concept in Ecclesiastes:

> Two are better than one, because they have a reward for their hard work. For if one of them should fail, the other

one can raise his partner up. But how will it be with just the one who falls where this is not another to raise him up?

We Americans are a pretty proud and individualistic bunch. We don't often like to admit weakness or accept help. Along with courage, it also takes great confidence and humility to admit where we need help.

> **Most businesses are mediocre. The goal is not to be more like business; the goal is to be great.**

Lastly, it is worth noting that this book will not argue that outsourcing is good because nonprofits need to be more run like businesses. As Jim Collins points out in his monograph, *Good to Great and the Social Sectors*, becoming more businesslike is not the goal. Most businesses are mediocre. The goal is not to be more like business; the goal is to be great.

Michael Edwards echoes this sentiment, in the November 28, 2011, *Wall Street Journal* article "Should Philanthropies Operate Like Businesses?" when he said, "Use business thinking only where it is appropriate. Stop the hype that surrounds the business-is-best approach."* Outsourcing is an appropriate strategy that, when correctly applied, can help the nonprofit sector.

The goal with this book is to begin to change the perceptions among capacity builders, funders, and nonprofit leaders. Outsourcing is not a dirty word. It is an organizational strategy that, when used effectively, can battle burnout, increase retention in our leadership, and achieve better outcomes.

As a result of my experiences over the past fifteen years, there are few who have thought as deeply or as often about outsourcing

---

*http://online.wsj.com/article/SB10001424052970204554204577024313200627678.html

in the nonprofit sector. I consider myself fortunate to have walked this journey. Mine is a niche within a niche, and I'm fortunate to be one of a handful of people in America who have spent considerable time and energy wrestling with these issues. It is my hope, as you read *Do What You Do Best*, that it will open your mind to new ways of improving our great sector.

OVERVIEW

THEORY OF OUTSOURCING AS CAPACITY BUILDING

"Capacity building" is the common term used to describe consulting and training for nonprofits. Capacity building, in the way of leadership training and professional development, is a very noble and needed goal. However, capacity building often goes too far. For example, executive directors need to know how to *analyze, understand, and use* financial information, but they don't necessarily need to know how to *create* it. In the past, technical capacity building efforts largely centered on the training and development of paid staff. There are some problems with this approach. For starters, many of those paid staff leave. Turnover is a significant issue in the sector. Another problem is that paid staff may not want to learn tedious skills like bookkeeping; they may want to focus on the mission and the programs. Or lastly, the organization may simply be too small to have access to all the skills it needs. And all the training in the world can't change these fundamental issues.

Capacity building was front and center in my mind after attending the Alliance for Nonprofit Management conference. It feels like there are over a hundred different definitions of capacity building and constant discussion around what it is exactly. However, strategic planning, executive coaching, financial training, and program evaluation all typically fall under the capacity building umbrella.

The conference hosted a discussion on "Financial Capacity Building—the Pieces of the Puzzle." Historically, funders and organizations that seek to help nonprofits have focused training efforts on how to *do* accounting. We believe that capacity building efforts should be focused on how to *use* accounting, not how to do accounting. Capacity building in the past has focused too much on getting everyone to do everything. I'm a big believer in the concept of teams and people focusing on what they do best. Not everyone can do everything, much less be good at it all.

> **The point of outsourcing is not to diminish capacity or to reduce spending, the focus is to ensure spending is done in the right place and done most efficiently.**

Financial capacity building is like a three-legged stool: without any leg the stool is a bit useless. When it comes to a nonprofit's finances, you need (1) a person or provider to *do* the work, (2) an executive director who can *use* the info, and (3) a board, chief financial officer (CFO), and/or treasurer who can *monitor* the process. Capacity building efforts, particularly around finance, should be focused on how to use and understand the information.

Can you imagine the Ohio Association of Plumbers hosting half-day Finance 101 workshops teaching folks how to use Quick-Books, training them on the nuances of cost accounting, explaining debits and credits, and then releasing them to go do all the work? Instead, realistically, they would teach them how to use financial information to determine their pricing, monitor cash flow, and budget for the future. The Association would teach them how to use the information and suggest to them they hire a bookkeeper, firm, or accountant to do the work. Plumbers understand intuitively that they are best at their labor, plumbing.

In *The World is Flat*, Thomas Friedman said, "They [the best companies] outsource to innovate faster and more cheaply in order to grow larger, gain market share, and hire more and different specialists." The point of outsourcing is not to diminish capacity or to reduce spending, the focus is to ensure spending is done in the right place and done most efficiently. The for-profit world talks about "gaining market share." In the nonprofit world that could translate into "more people helped" or "our cause advanced."

The notion of this book is to remove the negative label and stereotype that can come with outsourcing. Emotionally, when people hear "capacity building" it intrinsically feels good, and sounds worthy. Emotionally, when people hear "outsourcing" it sounds bad, evil, and corporate. The truth is somewhere in between. Outsourcing can be a useful strategy or tactic to help nonprofits build their capacity to do what they do best. Outsourcing is a great way to help leaders focus on their mission, their programs, and their passions.

OUTSOURCING VS. OFFSHORING
IS OUTSOURCING A DIRTY WORD?

In 2007 I visited Yellowstone National Park. Because of Yellowstone's unique ecosystem, there are nearly 300 environmental organizations in and around the park. Some former Yale students helped put together the Greater Yellowstone Conservation Directory. The goal was to simply catalog all the various groups, in the hopes that would then foster greater collaboration among the groups. It was a great place for me to test my own thesis concerning outsourcing, collaboration, and capacity building. I traveled there and met with about twenty of these organizations. Very quickly I learned that "outsourcing" was a long and dirty four-letter word. People would noticeably shut down and even become agitated if I used the word "outsourcing." I began my own little experiment. I would talk to them about any problems or challenges they faced. When a good vendor existed to help fill a particular need, I would share the info with the nonprofit's leader. If I described that vendor as a "professional services provider," people remained very open. If I described that vendor as an "outsourced partner," people shut down pretty quickly—even if it was the same vendor, with the same pricing, and the same benefits. Words do matter.

Although there is a movement in outsourcing circles to re-place the term, we've intentionally included the term "outsourcing" throughout this book to force the issue. Outsourcing can be about capacity build-ing, building greater programs, and helping others. Outsourcing is a tactic, a strategy that is neither good nor bad. This strategy, like most things in life, has pros and cons. It can be used for good purposes or for bad ones. But it, in and of itself, is not evil; it is simply a strategy.

> **Outsourcing can be about capacity building, building greater programs, and helping others.**

Furthermore, it is worthwhile to point out that outsourcing does not equal offshor-ing. Much to my chagrin, during the 2012 Presidential debate, candidates' messages and advertisements lamented the outsourcing movement in Amer-ica and used the term "outsourcing" to score political points. What they meant to attack, and what Americans are growing frustrated with, is offshoring. There is a significant difference between out-sourcing and offshoring.

Outsource — v. to move activities once performed by employees within the organization to a vendor outside of the organization.

Offshore — v. to outsource to a vendor located outside of one's home country.

When you hire someone to mow your lawn, you are outsourc-ing the care of your lawn to your neighbor's teenager. When you call Dell's help desk for technical support, you are likely talking to someone offshore in India.

Figure 1

SCOPE

	CAPTIVE OFFSHORING	OUTSOURCING & OFFSHORING
ACTIVITIES CONDUCTED IN OFFSHORE MARKETS	2	4
ACTIVITIES CONDUCTED IN LOCAL MARKETS	DOMESTIC INSOURCING	DOMESTIC OUTSOURCING
	1	3

ACTIVITIES CONDUCTED WITHIN THE COMPANY   ACTIVITIES CONDUCTED BY OUTSOURCING SUPPLIERS

Outsourcing—the topic of this book—does not necessarily include offshoring. Having lived and worked throughout Asia and having toured hundreds of factories throughout Asia, I have a unique perspective on offshoring. My in-laws also live in Michigan, one of the areas in the U.S. hardest hit by manufacturing offshoring. I also have extended family living in Mississippi in an area that has benefited from the opening of a Toyota plant. Globalization is complicated. In an increasingly globalized world, for better or worse, offshoring is here to stay. From a macro perspective, there are arguments among very smart people as to whether offshoring is good or bad for America, but most agree that offshoring and increased international trade is good for our world.

From a micro perspective, the newly employed worker in a Vietnamese factory is proud to be able to go home and provide for his family after a hard day's work. And for the factory worker laid off in Michigan, that employee may struggle to make ends meet and provide for his family. Even when something is good at the macro level, it certainly doesn't mean it isn't painful or difficult at the micro (i.e., personal) level. So while offshoring is certainly a complex topic, the focus of this book is on outsourcing.

Outsourcing is fundamentally about doing what you do best. If someone does something better than you, and you do something better than that person, you should help each other out. Economic geeks call this "comparative advantage."

COMPARATIVE ADVANTAGE
DO WHAT YOU DO BEST
AND OUTSOURCE THE REST

I'm a terrible cook. I can cook grilled cheese and burn hot dogs on the grill. That's about it. My wife, on the other hand, is a fantastic cook. My wife loves computers but is allergic to fixing them; I (sometimes) enjoy working on computers. So she cooks and I'm the information technology (IT) help desk at home. We focus on our comparative desires and strengths, and our family is better for it. Incidentally, we both hate to iron so we outsource that to the local dry cleaners. That also makes us a happier family.

The classic example of comparative advantage is trade between two factories.

The Idaho factory can produce five potatoes and two oranges per day. The Florida factory can produce three potatoes and four oranges per day. If the Idaho factory focuses just on potatoes, they can process ten potatoes per day. And the Florida factory can process eight oranges per day. When they agree to trade potatoes for oranges, the Idaho factory keeps five potatoes, but now gets four oranges. And the Florida factory now gets five potatoes and still keeps four oranges.

They are both better off; each now has more. In effect, they have outsourced part of their production to their neighbor, and it is

OVERVIEW

Figure 2

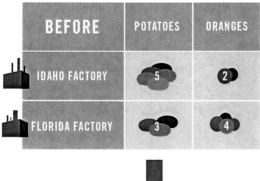

BEFORE	POTATOES	ORANGES
IDAHO FACTORY	5	2
FLORIDA FACTORY	3	4

FOCUSED PRODUCTION	POTATOES	ORANGES
IDAHO FACTORY	10	0
FLORIDA FACTORY	0	8

AFTER TRADE	POTATOES	ORANGES
IDAHO FACTORY	5	4
FLORIDA FACTORY	5	4

OVERVIEW

a classic win-win. They focused on what they did best—Idaho on potatoes and Florida on oranges—and they won.

Outsourcing within an organization relies on the exact same logic. Many nonprofit leaders are pioneers in their fields. They are inspirational social workers, artistic visionaries, and passionate advocates for their cause. They lead, motivate, and create. They are energized when they engage their mission. They are de-motivated and lose energy when they turn to the tedious tasks of accounting, complying with local human resources (HR) regulations, and ensuring their insurance coverage is up to date. Strangely, there are people in this world—like me—who receive energy taking care of the back-office tasks. We love being the support team and helping the people on the front lines.

> They lead, motivate, and create. They are energized when they engage their mission.

Can you imagine if we switched our team of accountants with the local corps de ballet? And we all performed each other's jobs for the day? Our accountants would cringe at the idea of being on a stage, in tights, attempting to keep the beat and appear graceful. We would surely sprain an ankle and bruise our egos. And most dancers would cringe at the idea of sitting behind a computer, adding up numbers, interpreting grant reports, and reconciling bank statements. They may not sprain an ankle, but they would certainly be frustrated and bored!

To use the same math as the generic potatoes and oranges example, if nonprofits focus on doing what they do best, more people will be helped and more positive outcomes achieved. For example, it may take a trained accountant ten hours to handle a small nonprofit's books each month. Therefore, in a normal 160 hour working month, the accountant could handle sixteen nonprofits. Those same nonprofits may not have the oversight and training for bookkeeping, so it takes them twenty hours a month on their books, or about twice as long. This means, across those sixteen nonprofits, they need the equivalent of two full-time people doing their books. When the single trained accountant is working, the nonprofits free up forty hours per week of time that can be devoted to programs and furthering the mission. In the perpetually under-resourced nonprofit sector, the more productivity we can gain from our existing resources, the better. Spread that ten hour per month savings across 1.2 million small and midsize nonprofits, and you've just done the equivalent of moving 75,000 people from administrative work into front-line program work. Granted the math is a bit more complicated than that, but through this simple example you can begin to see the magnitude of the opportunity. There is no doubt; outsourcing can increase the capacity of the nonprofit sector.

> **In the perpetually under-resourced nonprofit sector, the more productivity we can gain from our existing resources, the better.**

Outsourcing is all about doing what you do best. You can use outsourcing in your daily and professional lives, whether it's dry cleaning or accounting, to focus your time and energy on what you do best.

TYPES OF OUTSOURCING

OUTSOURCING IS NOT JUST FOR THE BACK OFFICE

Charity: water (www.charitywater.org) is a wildly popular nonprofit in the Gen-Y and Gen-X crowd. Its founder, Scott Harrison, is a former NYC nightclub promoter and he has transferred his publicity skills to become a leading charismatic figure in the nonprofit sector. Charity: water was an early adopter of Twitter and one of the first accounts to accumulate over a million followers. It throws some of the best galas in NYC and has an innovative fund-raising platform to connect donors with their wells. It has grown in just a few years to a $30+ million organization. Charity: water's mission is to provide clean drinking water to hundreds of thousands of people in the developing world. The funny thing is, charity: water doesn't drill wells. It doesn't employ engineers or geologists. An organization that has the sole mission and goal in life to provide clean drinking water doesn't have a single person on the payroll who drills wells. They outsource it all.

Charity: water is a young organization, having sprouted up in 2008. Early on, its founders realized that there were already people in the field, organizations that had been toiling with the African mud for decades. They knew the soil; they knew the weather patterns; they knew the water tables. Why would a bunch of trendy folks in NYC start trying to learn how to drill wells? They shouldn't. They should focus on engaging and inspiring millions of people (literally) to care about clean water and to give towards clean water projects. They realized that their biggest impact, and their biggest strength, lay in fundraising and inspiring. And they have been wildly successful at that, raising millions of dollars and increasing awareness among untold millions. They were smart enough to outsource the water projects—wells, rainwater harvesting systems, biosand filters, etc.—to others, allowing them to do what they do best.

Create Common Good (www.createcommongood.org) in Boise, Idaho, is another example of an organization that knows its role and place in the world. Create Common Good (CCG) provides training and employment to refugees and others in need. Their experiential programs transform lives by teaching others to fish and by bringing access to fresh, conveniently prepared, local food products. It has embraced outsourcing and is making an impact far greater than one would expect from an organization with an annual budget of less than $1 million. Refugees come to America through an established network of government agencies and nonprofits. These resettlement organizations work in tandem to provide refugees housing, health care, English training, and hopefully employment. Create Common Good observed this system and saw that the weak link in the chain was experiential job training. Refugees have wildly varying backgrounds when they arrive in America—PhDs from Bhutan alongside preliterate or innumerate folks from Somalia. Training such a diverse group, most who may struggle with English, can be a daunting challenge.

Create Common Good saw this niche, zeroed in on it, and now has an outstanding organization in place yielding strong quantifiable results. The existing resettlement agencies in Boise often send "their clients" to Create Common Good for training. These agencies recognized that CCG was doing something creative, innovative, and effective. Rather than build the same training, they outsource this piece of the resettlement puzzle to CCG. With its laser focus CCG, in turn, regularly communicates and works with these agencies on the refugees' larger needs. These organizations share the mutual goal of economic independence for America's newest community members. And because the agencies are working together, each focusing on its unique strength, the refugees in Boise are better equipped for self-sufficiency.

The Center for Collaborative Change (http://newarkchange.org) in Newark, New Jersey, is another example of an organization that embraces the concept of teamwork and each party doing what they do best. Newark became well known among many for Cory Booker, its charismatic mayor, and the significant donation made by Mark Zuckerburg, founder of Facebook, to Newark schools. The Center's mission is to improve the lives of the inhabitants of Newark, and see it become a place of "health, safety, and opportunity." With that mission, you might imagine it operates a health clinic, runs late night shuttle services, or provides job training for the unemployed. In fact, it does none of these things. But it empowers and enables all of these things. As the Center says on its website, "The Center's role in Newark is distinctive. By working closely with decision-makers, but not being responsible for day-to-day service delivery, the Center is uniquely situated to identify efforts within the community, government, and other institutions that can be synergized with one another for greater impact."

The Center recognizes what it does best—systematically analyzing the issues, bringing facts and data to teams of decision makers, and identifying solutions to fix broken systems. Piecemeal solutions will not solve Newark's problems. Collaboration, and each party doing what they do best, will.

> **In fact, it does none of these things. But it empowers and enables all of these things.**

OUTSOURCING YOUR
BACK OFFICE
THE DONOR'S PERSPECTIVE

Generally, when people speak of outsourcing they tend to think of the back office. The back office generally refers to tasks like bookkeeping and accounting, human resources, IT management, and other infrastructure-related tasks. These chunks of work often require the highest level of expertise and are most common across organizations. In the nonprofit sector, for better or worse, there is a focus on the ratio of revenue that goes to programs vs. fundraising and administrative costs. The average across all sectors and all size organizations is approximately 25 percent.

Figure 3

†

AVERAGE PROGRAM EXPENDITURES OF NONPROFITS, BY SUBSECTOR

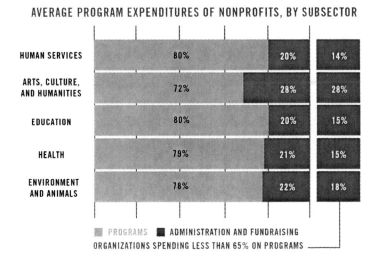

HUMAN SERVICES	80%	20%	14%
ARTS, CULTURE, AND HUMANITIES	72%	28%	28%
EDUCATION	80%	20%	15%
HEALTH	79%	21%	15%
ENVIRONMENT AND ANIMALS	78%	22%	18%

▨ PROGRAMS ■ ADMINISTRATION AND FUNDRAISING
ORGANIZATIONS SPENDING LESS THAN 65% ON PROGRAMS ⌐

We have heard from many nonprofits that they have been rejected for grants because their overhead costs were too high as a percentage of revenue. Organizations like Charity Navigator zealously monitor IRS 990 data and create scorecards based on this ratio. There is debate about what percentage of revenue spent on infrastructure support is appropriate. Everyone agrees that an organization that spends 70 percent of funds on administration is bordering on fraudulent. There is a general consensus that the more time, energy, and resources that go into programs, the better.

Yet it is also universally recognized that some level of organizational capacity and infrastructure is necessary to carry out the goals of the organization. We need accounting, board meetings, and fundraising. These can't be eliminated. But they can be streamlined and optimized so that our scarce dollars and time go further. Those

† NonProfit Overhead Cost Project: Center on Nonprofits and Philanthropy, Urban Institute; Center on Philanthropy, Indiana University

of us deep within the sector have discussions and arguments about what is the appropriate level. We know all the details, we know what it takes to run a nonprofit, and we care deeply and passionately. We want everyone to spend the time and energy to understand what it takes to run our nonprofits; we want them to know what is required. But our funders or our community may not care quite as deeply. A simple number is much easier to interpret. And research and data support that.

> The most cited reason, at seventy-four percent, was "I'd give more if less money were spent on administration."

In a poll, nearly half of all respondents (and sixty-two percent of wealthy respondents) said that they care how much nonprofits spend on administration and fundraising.[‡]

Nearly half of the respondents [when analyzing where they should give] focused on *how the organization uses its money*. In contrast, only 6 percent cited *fulfills a genuine need* or *makes a difference* as the primary reason for giving.[§]

In a separate survey, wealthy donors were asked, "What would it take for you to give more?" The most cited reason, at seventy-four percent, was "I'd give more if less money were spent on administration." The second most cited reason, at fifty-eight percent, was "I'd give more if I was able to determine impact of gifts."[¶]

So we can argue and attempt to change perceptions among donors. But the pragmatist in all of us knows that this will be a long-

---

‡ NonProfit Overhead Cost Project: Center on Nonprofits and Philanthropy, Urban Institute; Center on Philanthropy, Indiana University

§ NonProfit Overhead Cost Project: Center on Nonprofits and Philanthropy, Urban Institute; Center on Philanthropy, Indiana University

¶ Bank of America Study of High Net-Worth Philanthropy; Center of Philanthropy at Indiana University, 2006

term, time-consuming endeavor. Progress has been made on this front over the past ten years and more progress is needed, but the program-to-admin ratio is here to stay. Given that, practical organizations are wise to focus on their program-to-admin ratio and to use reasonable methods to ensure this ratio is appropriate.

Figure 4

BEFORE

Outsourcing can help organizations reduce their administrative expense and overhead. The Boy Scouts of America (BSA) just did an internal nationwide study proving that the more money it spent on district executives—employees on the front lines engaging the community, executing programs, fundraising, and working directly with the troops—the more its membership grew. The same cannot be said for money spent on bookkeepers and accountants. Furthermore, as BSA increases the monies spent on district executives, its membership grows, along with its outreach and impact. Focusing money on programs is a virtuous cycle, and is the reason nonprofits should exist.

TYPES OF BACK-OFFICE OUTSOURCING

There are all types of back-office outsourcing. There are organizations like Orr Associates (OAI), located in Washington, DC, that provide outsourced development. They are slightly different from fundraising consultants in that they actually do much of the legwork involved in development and fundraising. Because of strict fundraising rules, they do not solicit funds—that is the work of the client organization—but they prepare all the call lists, maintain the databases, coordinate the events, and more. Another group, Laurence A. Pagnoni & Associates (LAPA) in New York City, serves as a back office for fundraising to small and midsize nonprofits, as well as providing consulting for major campaigns.

More common are IT, HR, and accounting outsourcing. With the rise of cloud computing, the cost to outsource IT has decreased significantly. Technology applications and computer support have become more accessible and less expensive, regardless of your organization's size. At Jitasa, with just over fifty employees as of the summer of 2012, we outsource our IT support to the same company that provides IT support to Disney. Technology platforms and systems have become more uniform and accessible for organizations of all sizes. We gain the benefit of its scale and expertise in dealing with Disney, and it is able to leverage that same platform to help organizations with just a few employees and to help organizations with thousands. Another organization, Office Prodigy, has developed an innovative model in northern New England to provide outsourced PC support and an IT help desk for nonprofits throughout the region. Servers, LANS, Internet connections, Microsoft applications, Mac applications, and cloud-based applications all can be monitored and maintained remotely. No longer does each nonprofit need IT staff on its payroll. Nor does it need an "accidental techie"—a term for the beloved staff member who may not be trained but simply "is the most technical person around." That person often becomes the default expert in small organizations. Again, these people are well intentioned and do their best. But with an Internet connection and a very low, reasonable fee per computer, you can gain access to experts who can maintain your IT and infrastructure in a fraction of the time—and often with far better results.

> **HR compliance is like insurance: you don't know you need it until it is too late.**

In human resources (HR) outsourcing, payroll has been a widely accepted outsourced function for decades. It is an example of how specialization is a great reason and rationale for outsourcing. Payroll is a complex task with stringent IRS rules on taxes and withholdings. Building up that specific expertise can take years. Payroll companies already have this expertise. This is an area where many organizations comfortably outsource. HR benefit procurement and HR benefits management are other typical targets for outsourcing.

The Center for Nonprofit Advancement in Washington, DC, provides ways for nonprofits to join together to source their medical benefits, providing most members significant savings over doing it themselves. ADP, the world's leading provider of payroll services has created a "411" service that provides hotline support to organizations that have detailed legal HR questions. ADP processes one out of every six paychecks in America. HR rules and regulations are complex and ever shifting. Having an expert on call who can answer tricky questions about terminations or potential lawsuits can be incredibly valuable. HR compliance is like insurance: you don't know you need it until it is too late.

Finance and accounting outsourcing is probably the most common form of outsourcing among nonprofits.

Donald Packham, a member of Jitasa's board of directors, is widely considered the father of HR outsourcing. While working as a senior vice president at British Petroleum (BP), he outsourced all of HR at BP in a landmark and wildly successful outsourcing agreement. He went on to work as the chief human resources officer at the Federal Bureau of Investigation (FBI) and put many of those same principles to work.

Don believes that HR outsourcing providers are just now beginning to understand the scale and needs of the nonprofit sector. Outsourcing at the FBI or BP is very different from a twenty-person nonprofit, but HR outsourcing solutions are becoming less expensive and more accessible. And more and more nonprofits show an increased willingness to accept outsourcing as an option.

Finance and accounting outsourcing is probably the most common form of outsourcing among nonprofits. Outsourcing is an outgrowth from the need for specialization. Nonprofit accounting is much more complex than for-profit accounting. It includes all the rules of Generally Accepted Accounting Principles (GAAP) with another whole layer of nonprofit-specific rules and complexity wrapped around it. Ask a pizza shop owner what percentage of his cash is restricted and he would simply give you a blank stare or very clearly tell you that none of it is restricted—he can do whatever he wants with it! But nonprofit leaders have to wrestle with funding restrictions, reimbursable grants, grant reports, special-event accounting, and more. A 2008 survey of more than 300 nonprofits by a group of Yale students found finance and accounting to be the number one area nonprofits would be open and willing to outsource. The need for specialization drives this intuitive knowledge that outsourcing could be helpful.

> **Outsourcing is not simply about cost savings. It is about access to expertise.**

Jitasa, a provider of outsourced finance and accounting, conducts annual client satisfaction surveys. Clients consistently list "access to expertise" as the number one reason they hired Jitasa. Outsourcing is not simply about cost savings. It is about access to expertise and finding the specialized skills necessary for the complex world of nonprofit bookkeeping and accounting. I often refer to the "lonely bookkeeper syndrome." Most nonprofits simply do not have the scale necessary to support a five-person accounting department. To do so would be cost prohibitive. So the lonely bookkeepers do their best, working to understand and comply with the complexities of nonprofit bookkeeping. When a question comes up, who can they ask? The treasurer is often not a good option; statistically speaking she is not likely to be a CPA, but more likely to be the most "business-y" person on the board. The executive director is more likely to be a counselor or therapist than a CPA. The "lonely bookkeeper," no matter how well intentioned, lacks the expertise necessary and has no one to ask.

Figure 5 was also produced from the 2008 Yale survey:

Figure 5

TOP REASONS NONPROFITS CHOOSE
TO OUTSOURCE BACK-OFFICE SERVICES

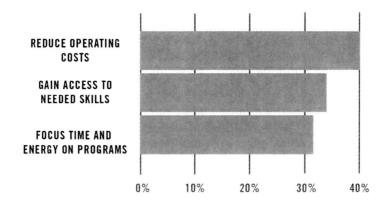

As one can see, saving money can be a key driver, but gaining access to needed skills and saving time are nearly equal reasons to outsource. A good back-office outsourcing provider should be able to achieve two, if not all three of these goals. In other cases, an organization may move to outsource based on one of these being the primary driver, only to realize all three benefits over time.

OUTSOURCING YOUR SPACE

Paying rent is a form of outsourcing. This is an example of outsourcing that most of us employ all the time—but perhaps we wouldn't call it outsourcing. Folks are choosing to have a vendor, the landlord, provide them space, maintenance, working bathrooms, and so forth instead of having janitors and maintenance employees on their own payroll. In exchange, the organization pays rent. It is a win-win. Rather than have ten buildings run by ten organizations, we have one landlord housing ten tenants in a building. This is less expensive for each organization and less expensive for society. It is another classic win-win, but one that we take for granted because it is so commonplace. The exact same theory and benefits apply when we outsource other parts of our organization.

Most organizations don't have the luxury of owning their buildings, so rent is a natural part of the picture. Jitasa began in a business incubator—an old warehouse renovated by the city of Boise to provide low-cost rent for start-ups. We were able to pay modest rent and immediately have a furnished place, a receptionist, a copier, Internet, and access to conference rooms. It was a great place to start. We now are in a larger office building, paying rent. The landlord does all the maintenance and janitorial services.

There are organizations, like the Tides Foundation or Marin Space, that provide shared spaces for nonprofits. One of the Tides

Foundation's programs, the Nonprofit Centers Network is dedicated to providing shared multi-tenant nonprofit centers and other quality nonprofit workspaces.

Many communities have areas where nonprofits congregate. There is an office building in Bozeman, Montana, at the front door of Yellowstone National Park where every other door is a different environmental nonprofit group. By sharing space they are more likely to share ideas, collaborate on programs, and avoid duplication of research in the park. Collectively outsourcing to the same spot yields them all collective benefits that no single organization could get on its own. By creating these shared physical spaces, they go beyond the simple benefit of renting vs. buying; they also increase the interaction of staff through the course of the day's normal activities.

BIG vs. SMALL

Outsourcing can help organizations of any size. Jitasa helps clients who range in size from a $100 million or larger annual budget to organizations who spend less than $50,000 each year. Brand name, nationally federated organizations comprised of a bunch of smaller chapters, councils, or affiliates are also great candidates for the value of outsourcing. Organizations with "scale" may decide to focus strategically on transformational change—focusing solely on their core competencies. It may not be a matter of expertise, but a matter of time and focus of organizational energy. A good outsourcing provider should continue to innovate, lower costs, and drive efficiencies into the process. At Jitasa, we often take the best practices from one of our more than 200 clients and apply them to the rest. Outsourcing providers are in a unique position to provide these types of intangible benefits that do not show up on a spreadsheet. Organizations of all sizes can benefit from outsourcing.

BENEFITS FOR NONPROFITS, LARGE OR SMALL

In the nonprofit world, the terms "large" and "small" are often skewed. A mid-market business may be a $500-million-dollar-a-year company. In the nonprofit world, outside of hospitals and higher education, that would be considered huge. About 90 percent of nonprofits have less than $1 million in annual revenues. This means they probably have five to fifteen staff members. That, from my view, makes about 90 percent of the nonprofit world "small" as it relates to organizational scale.

Larger organizations that have "achieved scale" still benefit greatly from outsourcing. It is no accident that Fortune 500 companies were the first to realize the benefits of outsourcing. Glenn Davidson, a Jitasa advisor and national expert in public sector outsourcing, recently remarked that he felt nonprofits are just beginning their journey to accept outsourcing. He remarked that he's seen a significant difference in attitudes in the nonprofit sector between 2007 and 2011.

Figure 6 from Equaterra Outsourcing Advisors, now part of consulting giant KPMG, reveals the same trend. As the technology becomes more accessible, as more vendors and social entrepreneurs seek to serve nonprofits, and as the concept becomes more

Figure 6

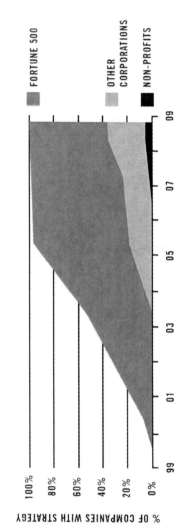

IMPLEMENTATION OF OUTSOURCING / OFFSHORE STRATEGY

FORTUNE 500

OTHER
CORPORATIONS

NON-PROFITS

% OF COMPANIES WITH STRATEGY

100%
80%
60%
40%
20%
0%

99   01   03   05   07   09

ACCORDING TO EQUATERRA OUTSOURCING ADVISORS, NPs ARE JUST NOW BEGINNING TO
ADOPT THE OUTSOURCING STRATEGIES PREVIOUSLY IMPLEMENTED BY CORPORATIONS.

widely accepted, more and more nonprofits will outsource. Much like nonprofits were slower to adapt integrated enterprise level ERP (enterprise resource planning) software systems, nonprofits are proving to lag behind in outsourcing acceptance. All indications suggest a significant increase in outsourcing as an accepted practice in the nonprofit industry.

It is also worth noting, that although Fortune 500 companies have plenty of "scale," they zealously pursued the benefits of outsourcing. In 1996 I worked on a project with Accenture dedicated to outsourcing all of DuPont's IT. Accenture put 200 people on the project for six weeks, and that was just to put together the proposal. In the end, DuPont outsourced all of its IT to two different providers, which at that point in 1996 was the largest outsourcing IT deal to date. British Petroleum outsourced most of its HR for its tens of thousands of employees. These, and all the rest of the Fortune 500, chose to outsource because they wanted to focus on what they did best.

> It was not a matter of achieving scale.
> It was a matter of organizational focus.

DuPont wanted to focus on its plants' operational efficiency and its research and development. Management did not care who maintained its Microsoft Office licenses on its PCs around the globe. British Petroleum wanted to focus on oil exploration, safety in its operations, and research into alternative energies. BP executives didn't want to spend time managing health benefits, unemployment claims, and so forth. They wanted to focus on doing what they did best. Or perhaps, what they wanted to do best. By getting out of the business of IT and HR benefits management, these organizations would divert that time and energy into things that would truly help their mission.

The same is true for large nonprofits. World Vision is based just outside of Seattle, Washington, but has employees and operations around the world. It has set up a service center in Manila, Philippines, to help analyze and make sense of the volumes of data accumulated around the world. As an international development organization, locating in Manila was not a philosophical stretch and fit within its mission. By centralizing talent in Manila, World Vision is able to train one group of about thirty people to help offices worldwide. These offices contain over 40,000 employees and have a collective budget of over $2 billion. World Vision realized that it would increase its ability to analyze and interpret data by creating a "Center of Excellence" in Manila. The center has created standard processes and has trained people on how to download and interpret data, and how to summarize that for management. It provides monthly reports to managers worldwide, relying on consistent data.

World Vision's primary goal in creating this shared service center was not cost savings, but was improved quality. Although labor is less expensive in Manila than in the U.S., it is actually more expensive than in some of the other countries where World Vision operates.

Jitasa works with a large museum in New York City that has over 1,000 employees. It has plenty of scale. However, it is really busy over the December holiday season and is really busy in the summer. Even with all that scale and with more than thirty people in the accounting department, the museum struggled to handle the variations in demand. Ramping staff up and down was difficult. Bringing in temporary bookkeepers, training them on the complex Oracle ERP system, only to see them leave a few weeks later was increasingly frustrating—and costly. An outsourced partner was needed who could ramp up or down quickly based on the peaks in demand. At the time, Jitasa had about 150 clients, all with different periods of high and low activity.

Although this museum was large and had "scale," Jitasa as an outsourced provider had a different kind of scale. We could spread the work across multiple clients with different seasonality— from Boy Scout summer camps to schools with little activity in the summer. It is a classic outsourcing win-win. We could provide the service cheaper than the museum could on its own because of our own workload. Now the museum has the consistency of a single provider and the flexibility to ramp up or down as its needs dictate.

Franchised or affiliated nonprofits are another example of "bigger than small" nonprofits. These are the groups that have a national brand, but usually have unique 501(c)(3)s serving local geographies. Groups like the YMCA, Boy Scouts of America, Make*A*Wish, Special Olympics, and many more have this model. Some have moved towards centralized national or regional service centers, some have outsourced all or a portion of their back office, and some remain primarily decentralized. Many of these organizations were founded decades ago, or in some cases, more than 100 years ago. At the time, decentralization was about the only way to operate a national model. The airplane was just being invented when the Boy Scouts was founded and organized. Now, with the advent of airplanes and technology, nonprofits have choices regarding which model they choose. There are many great studies that outline the pros and cons of centralization, the best coming from Yale's School of Management Professor Sharon Oster (http://mba.yale.edu/faculty/profiles/oster.shtml).

One thing in the research is pretty consistent: shared services make sense for most organizations. The program impact and cultural impact is often minimal and the financial savings and quality improvements are significant. That is money that can be saved and diverted into programs and mission critical activities. Shared services, or outsourcing as a group to a vendor, is a quick way to achieve financial savings across an affiliated network, improve

OUTSOURCING VS. SHARED SERVICES VS. MERGERS

Mergers and consolidation have long been a topic of conversation in nonprofit circles. There has been an explosion of nonprofits in America, with estimates ranging from 1.4 to 1.6 million organizations, approximately one for every 250 Americans. I've been to plenty of nonprofit conferences where nonprofit leaders and board members wax philosophical about the need for collaboration or consolidation. "We should all work together, sharing office space, bookkeepers, and admin assistants." "Perhaps we should merge!" "Why does this community need three youth advocacy organizations?" All the leaders at the round table undoubtedly will nod their head in enthusiastic agreement.

That's when I enjoy asking, "OK, excellent. So who will organize and lead it?" Everyone shrinks away and avoids making eye contact. It is like the childhood story of the hen and her bread. The hen asks the other animals to help her collect the grain, thresh the grain, prepare the dough, and bake the bread. No one wants to help. Then when it comes time to eat the bread, all the other animals want to share in the hen's hard work. The challenge with collaboration is the same—everyone wants the benefits, but no one wants to do the work.

Outsourcing solves this issue of "initiation energy." It takes a lot of time and energy to initiate a merger or shared service. There are countless decisions to be made, processes to be developed, possibly technology to be implemented. There are time-consuming and incredibly difficult decisions to be made around personnel, board structure, and more. Someone has to spend considerable time to lead and guide this effort. Someone has to initiate the process. When people outsource and chose a proven vendor partner, the provider has already built all the systems and processes. They have the checklists developed and they can walk you through the implementation. They can help each organization individually achieve scale, improve their quality, and focus on what it does best.

The challenge with collaboration is the same— everyone wants the benefits, but no one wants to do the work.

Mergers and shared services are *hard* work. You need committed boards, egoless leaders, a dedicated project manager, a team of lawyers, consensus on the details, and a governance structure, to name a few hurdles. There are many great examples of successful mergers, and untold stories of mergers gone awry. The national office of the Boy Scouts of America regularly facilitates mergers among the 300 councils in America. The national office provides outstanding support, project plans, and direction. Even with that strong and somewhat neutral advocate, the mergers can be really tough. For example, when you are merging two neighboring Boy Scout councils, and both have board members and employees who have been dedicated to the cause of scouting for more than twenty years, how do you choose whom to ask to leave? The pain of those decisions can often outweigh the financial benefits of the merger. These are difficult issues and most nonprofits have neither the benefit of Boy Scout's scale, nor its 100 years of experience dealing with these issues.

The Tides Foundation came out with "Shared Services: a Guide to Creating Collaborative Solutions" in 2010 that can be found on its website, www.nonprofitcenters.org. This study outlines how organizations can benefit from shared services and back-office collaboration. It goes on to list how nonprofits can collaborate to create their own shared service centers. It can be used as a workbook on how to set up shared services, which is largely defined as collaboration among existing nonprofit entities. It is a great body of work, well researched, and certainly will be useful to some within the sector. But as you read it and scan the worksheets and sample project plans, you can quickly be overwhelmed by the sheer energy, effort, and potential pitfalls of going down this path. The guide also points out that the "costs of setting up a complex shared services program can be substantial." There is an entire section on how costs should be allocated between the various collaborators and partners. These are all very complex and real issues. The Meyer Foundation report on outsourcing supports this notion when it reports:

Shared services, except in the context of fiscal sponsorship arrangements, appear extremely difficult to sustain. Many service providers and nonprofit sector experts interviewed for this study say that while all parties to shared services arrangements "want the benefits of the shared resource, no one wants to run it, implement it, or have ownership of it." These arrangements fall apart on issues of "turf and personalities," and on technical, legal, and psychological barriers—questions of who is in control, who owns the data, and of fairness in the allocation of the shared resource's time and attention. Even when users in shared service arrangements enter with high trust, clear contracts, and great expectations, their energy for maintaining and governing the shared service arrangement seems to decay over time. As one well-informed and experienced provider of back-office services put it, "we hope the nonprofit sector will just skip this step of shared services and move to the better solution of outsourcing from the start."

It is worth noting, that many Fortune 500 companies started by establishing shared service centers to support their various divisions. Over time, as their divisions warred over cost allocations and decreasing service levels, these organizations decided to move to an outsourcing relationship. Genpact, once owned by GE, is an example of a company that started as an internal service center. GE ultimately decided to spin it off into its own separate entity, and thus avoid the complications in a complex inter-dependent shared service relationship and instead enjoy the clarity of a client-vendor relationship. Its website, www.genpact.com, says:

> Genpact has a unique heritage, which has contributed to our deep understanding of process. We began in 1997 as a business unit within GE, building the Company from the ground up. Our charter was to provide business process services to GE's businesses, with the goal of enabling outstanding efficiencies. During the eight years that followed, we earned the opportunity to manage a wide range of processes from the simple to complex, operating across GE's financial-services and manufacturing businesses. In January 2005, we became an independent company bringing our process expertise and unique DNA in Lean Six Sigma to clients outside the GE family. Our new name, Genpact, conveys the business impact we generate for our clients.

It is much easier to fire a poorly performing vendor than it is to deal with a poorly performing internal service center. The internal service center has to make decisions such as "Do I serve division A or division B today?" or "How much more should I request to add to my budget?" In an outsourcing relationship, this is the vendor's problem. The vendor has to manage competing priorities: risking price increases against the risk of client attrition, or pricing higher than the competition.

Many well-intentioned initiatives in the nonprofit sector—typically driven by a funder or group of funders—attempt to get shared service centers or collaborative arrangements in place. Most of these die on the vine due to complex cost allocation agreements, issues around initiation energy, and the ultimate governance structure.

Outsourcing makes these issues go away. An outsourcing partner has figured out all these issues once and all of its clients benefit. Can you imagine creating an accounting shared service center, staffed with fifty accountants and CPAs, and then convincing 200 nonprofits to come together to collaborate on the cost and time allocations and work processes of that center? It would take forever and likely never get off the ground. However, this is exactly what Jitasa built from 2008 to 2011. All 200 nonprofits didn't have to agree and come together at the exact same time and they are spread out all over the country. They came to us over a period of three to four years and each made its own independent decisions. But together, they all reaped the same benefits of a shared service arrangement. Shared services and collaboration can be a strategy that works in unique circumstances, but outsourcing is also a viable—and potentially even more beneficial—strategy.

Jan Masaoka, the editor of Blue Avocado, wrote a great article in September 2011 called "Only Bad Restaurants Go to Scale" (http://blueavocado.org/content/only-bad-restaurants-go-scale). Jan is and has been a thought leader in the nonprofit sector for a long time. She offers a dispassionate, grounded view on much of the conventional wisdom in our sector. In this article, she describes that the "cost per unit produced" often goes up with a merger, not down. For example, if two $1-million nonprofits that don't currently require an audit merge, the new entity may require an audit. And that makes the new entity actually more expensive, not less expensive. She notes, "In economics this is called the problem of increasing—rather than declining—marginal costs. Here's a simple way to see it: in a factory you can get a machine to produce twice as many products with only 1.5 times the cost. But you can't get a social worker to do that. In fact, a large organization has to invest in quality control and complex personnel systems that a small organization can manage just by looking around."

> There is a certain "optimal scale" for nonprofits.

However, the *intention* behind mergers and shared services is wise. Eighty percent of nonprofits are really small, with annual revenue of less than $100,000. Another 10 percent are less than $1 million in revenue. All of these organizations require a board of directors, an accounting function, an HR function, insurance policies, IT infrastructure, and more. It would be somewhat silly, or cost prohibitive, for each of these tiny organizations to build this entire infrastructure by themselves. There is a certain "optimal scale" for nonprofits. With too few resources, small nonprofits are sort of frozen into inaction. Too big, and nonprofits stop being niche fillers in society, increase their cost per person served, and potentially lose touch with the people they help. Overall, however, nonprofits fill needed and necessary niches in society, therefore we want nonprofits of all sizes to survive and thrive. TIME magazine reported in a November 2011 article on U.S. poverty that:

> The research outfit MDRC has spent decades evaluating dozens of anti-poverty programs, and as its president, Gordon Berlin says, "We're seeing a growing body of evidence that the things that work tend to be small in scale."

Small can be beautiful, and the data is starting to show that too. Small done right, done smartly, truly helps society.

Outsourcing provides nonprofits another option to achieve scale, without sacrificing their nimble nature. For a smaller organization that has chosen a particular niche of the sector, the need to focus time, energy, and resources is even more amplified. When you are under-resourced, it becomes even more necessary to find your comparative strengths and to zealously focus.

Organizations don't have to merge, or even collaborate with their nonprofit brethren, to achieve scale. They can outsource their non-core functions and zero in on the one to two things where they truly excel. When our sector can harness and capture that human potential, freeing up millions to focus on their passions, we will be able to see even more return for our hard work, time, and tears.

> **Small can be beautiful, and the data is starting to show that too.**

Outsourcing solves many of the problems associated with mergers. When you outsource, you are choosing a vendor partner. The relationship is very clear. You hired the firm to help. They have service levels to achieve and performance targets to hit. In a merger, especially one of relative equals, the relationship is not clear. Who has what decision-making authority? Who is doing what in the new world? And it takes a lot of time and energy to think through all of these issues and to resolve them. Outsourcing avoids almost all of this.

Another recurring issue with mergers and collaboration, unfortunately, often comes down to egos or job security. Previously you had two board presidents, two executive directors, and two directors of programs. In the merged entity, you now just need one of each. Although most all of us in the sector are genuinely interested in the greater good, when it comes down to our own job and us personally, it is a little harder to be the one who steps away. Outsourcing avoids this issue. It provides groups with scale, without having to eliminate leadership positions of paid staff and volunteers.

No doubt there is a time and place for mergers. But that is not the single solution. One hundred percent of Fortune 500 companies outsource, but not all are rushing into mergers. Mergers will not necessarily solve the "problem of scale," and a lot of time and energy is required to pull them off successfully. And no doubt there is a need for collaboration in our sector. However, collaboration is just a less formal version of a merger. Collaboration still requires significant alignment of values, goals, and egos. Collaboration requires significant initiation energy, and it requires someone to take the lead. Collaboration is a beautiful thing properly executed. Outsourcing can be too.

COMMON
CONCERNS

TIME VS. MONEY

Generally in nonprofits, money is more scarce than time. It is always possible to work a little longer or find a volunteer. It is not always possible to have more money available. So decision makers in nonprofits naturally gravitate towards the resource that they have more of—time—and make decisions accordingly.

This can lead to the trap of thinking that outsourcing isn't feasible, because it costs money. Often in small, overworked organizations the idea of paying for an additional line item in the budget is simply impossible. The logic follows that saving an executive director's time is nice, but she is going to work sixty hours a week anyway. Having a bookkeeping firm help out so that she works fifty hours a week only adds to the budget; it doesn't save money. This is a very real and valid argument. However, when played out over the long run, this is a death trap. It creates a system that relies on overworked people and relies on their continued relentless dedication to your cause. MIT sociologist, Oliver Hahl, describes the Law of Diminishing Intrinsic Return, which states that eventually people's dedication dies off over time because they are doing things they don't enjoy—such as bookkeeping—that take them away from their mission. So while your—probably unstated—strategy is to rely on people's dedication, you are setting up a system where their dedication will undoubtedly wane over time. This creates burnout and turnover, two expensive issues that nonprofits regularly face. This downward spiral can be avoided by allowing people to focus on what they enjoy and do best.

The Meyer Foundation's report in 2009, titled "Outsourcing Back-Office Services in Small Nonprofits: Pitfalls and Possibilities," accurately reported:

> For those organizations most in need of better back-office services, outsourcing may not offer short-term cost savings, but can offer significant long-term benefits and savings. Nonprofits that are spending very little to perform a function poorly won't save money by transferring it to an outside firm. However, the long-term benefits and cost savings could be significant if outsourcing means the Executive Director and other key staff can spend more time on program and strategy and they are less distracted by important work for which they have little time or training (or by the serious and sometimes costly consequences of neglecting back-office functions).

As with most things in life, there are tradeoffs that need to be considered between the short-term and the long-term.

People who run youth advocacy organizations typically love working with youth. They are energized when counseling youth, playing alongside them, or helping them find their way in the world. They lose energy when forced to discuss budgets, insurance policies, or HR compliance issues. This became incredibly evident to me as I was talking with Christine Jackson, an executive director serving youth (note: not her real name). Her organization ran an amazing national program that takes inner-city children and provides them an upper-class summer school experience. The children learn life skills and also hard skills such as reading and arithmetic, helping to close the achievement gap. This achievement gap persists across socioeconomic boundaries and countless research shows that summer school plays a role. When I talked with Christine, you could see her eyes light up and hear the enthusiasm in her voice as she talked about the program's results. She could name students and remember details of their experiences from years before. She rattled off statistics and studies done by researchers investigating the achievement gap over the years. Then when I asked her to tell me about her financial performance and her annual budget, her entire demeanor changed. She averted her eyes for a bit, shoulders slumped ever so slightly, and she began to answer my questions. Her voice inflection and tone flattened as she mechanically told me about revenues and expenses. Further in the conversation she admitted that she didn't enjoy this area and went on to say, "When I talk to our bookkeeper, it feels like the blind leading the blind." And Christine had an MBA, so she was much more prepared than most of our nonprofit leaders. I see this all the time across the nonprofits we serve. Executive directors who are passionate and clearly motivated by a cause are de-motivated by the chores of organizational structure required to achieve those goals.

Christine recognized this in herself and had the self-awareness to begin to think strategically regarding the best use of her time—in the short and long term—and she began to embrace back-office outsourcing. She wanted to increase the number of summer school partners in the program's network. Each school added greatly increased the access in that local area for the lower socioeconomic children to enjoy a summer school experience. Donors funded her passion. They funded her results. And they wanted stable, accurate, well-controlled finances. Christine realized that her passion and her knowledge of programs were her strengths—and her passion. When she was in her own personal sweet spot, the organization would thrive. If she deviated and tried to do too much on her own, her true talents and passions would be marginalized.

Outsourcing is a way to ensure that our nonprofit leaders are in their sweet spot. Outsourcing is a way to minimize the energy and effort required to create organizational structure. And outsourcing is a way for us to help our selfless nonprofit leaders stay motivated.

Board members who worry about succession planning and leader retention should investigate outsourcing as a way to keep our nonprofit leaders motivated.

> **Board members who worry about succession planning and leader retention should investigate outsourcing as a way to keep our nonprofit leaders motivated.**

The "Daring to Lead 2006" study by CompassPoint and the Meyer Foundation cited "limited management infrastructure and lack of administrative support as key contributors to executive director burnout and turnover." Allowing our leaders to focus on what they do best, we get our organizations out of the downward death spiral and into an upward virtuous spiral. When our leaders are motivated and energized, those around them feed off that energy. Society benefits when our leaders are engaging the community, fundraising, and improving their programs.

Our nonprofit leaders are passionate people, we—as a sector—should help them focus on what they do best. When they can spend their time on the things they enjoy most, they will be most productive and their organizations will produce better outcomes.

WILL I LOSE CONTROL?

The number one reason organizations do not want to outsource is for a perceived lack of control. Data among Fortune 500 companies nearly perfectly match the research done with nonprofits by a group of Yale students in 2008:

Figure 7

WHAT ARE THE TOP TWO REASON NON-PROFITS CHOOSE NOT TO OUTSOURCE OR PARTNER WITH ANOTHER ORGANIZATION TO PROVIDE BACK-OFFICE SERVICES?

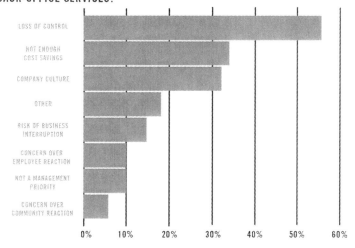

Control is a very real issue. However it is largely an issue of perception. As Laurence A. Pagnoni wrote in an article on the topic (http://www.capabilitycompany.com/articles/articlenpoutsourcing.shtm):

Some nonprofit executives, for example, are prejudiced by one unsatisfactory experience with a consultant. They freeze-frame that experience and replay it in their memory and stop themselves from hiring another consultant who might be capable of doing a fine job. Is dismissing someone for poor performance a barrier to hiring new staff? Why then should an experience with an inept consultant form a barrier to engaging another?

In this case, there is an idea that with an employee we have the ability to control them, find them, hire them, and replace them, as necessary. Anyone who has ever managed employees knows this is not true! Nor so simple! Employees frequently don't follow their boss's orders; they forget to show up on time; before termination they must receive multiple official warnings from HR; and on it goes. Control over an employee is a façade. It is much easier to fire a consultant or a vendor than an employee. So, although there is a perceived feeling of a lack of control, in some cases you actually increase your control by working with an outside party.

Later in the article, Mr. Pagnoni goes on to report:

"There is a concern that they [local governments] lost control, even though governments that outsource have found that they actually gain control." Savas [Presidential Professor of the School of Public Affairs at Baruch College] has studied government outsourcing to nonprofits in eight major cities and is the author of *Privatization*, a seminal work on the subject.

Stephen Goldsmith, the former mayor of Indianapolis, outsourced some eighty functions including water plants, solid-waste—i.e., garbage-disposal and street paving. He said, "I have more control over private contractors than I ever had over my own work force!"

A good outsourced vendor has certain performance targets to meet, and is driven and motivated to ensure those targets are met.

There are certainly examples of outsourcing providers who provide lousy service, lock their clients into horrible long-term contracts, and abdicate responsibility. Care must be taken when setting up the initial contract. Some vendors offer clients the ability to terminate services at any time for any reason with thirty-day notice. That provides clients a lot of flexibility and provides the vendor with plenty of incentive to make sure to continuously deliver value to the clients.

Another typical area of control is around data. Does the non-profit own the data or does the outsourced provider? Good vendors will allow their clients to own their own data. Vendors should not hold clients' data hostage, while providing lousy service. This is another area that should be considered during the initial contract phase.

Another example of increased control vs. a lack of control can be found in how the arrangements are set up. ADP offers a tax payment guarantee. If they fail to pay your payroll taxes, ADP pays all IRS fines and penalties. If your in-house payroll experts made that mistake, you legally would not be allowed to ask them to pay the fines, nor could you dock their pay. Nor would it cross any reasonable person's mind to ask one's own employees to pay for a mistake.

> **Again, this actually gives nonprofits more control than if they were using their own staff.**

Your only recourse would be to fire them, and that also seems awfully strict for one mistake. But outsourcing partners oftentimes pay for their mistakes. **Again, this actually gives nonprofits more control than if they were using their own staff.**

The last example of this concerns the control and knowledge of the activities of staff. At Jitasa, we track our employees' activities in six-minute increments. All of their time is available to clients in their unique client portal via the Internet. Clients can see, in real time, exactly how much time any associate is spending on their account for any given task. A client recently remarked to me, "I know more about what you all do than I ever knew about our in-house book-keeper. You all are 1,500 miles away and she sat in the office next to me! I didn't know if she was doing AP or Facebook. I didn't know if AP should take ten hours a week or thirty." A good outsourced provider should be able to provide you with clear transparency into the work and activities on your account. If a provider is unwilling to provide complete transparency, keep looking for a better option.

Control is a very real concern. However, for the most part, it comes down to perceptions vs. facts. Choosing the right partner is key in this regard. Ensure that your original contract gives you the control and transparency you need. And often, when analyzed closely, you will find that you actually increase your level of control when working with the right outsourced provider.

DO I NEED TO GET MY HOUSE IN ORDER FIRST?

As a child, my mom used to always tell the four of us kids to clean our rooms because today she was going to clean the house. We often joked that we didn't understand why we needed to clean our room to prepare for our room to be cleaned. Now, twenty-five years later, I'm married and my wife tells me the same thing! Clearly the intention is to get the house in order so that someone can vacuum and dust without having to weave through my books, toys, and clothes lying around. Outsourcing is sort of the same. The house doesn't have to be clean in order to outsource, but the owner of the house does have some obligation to help the process along.

Some organizations may choose to migrate functions to a vendor, and then transform. Others transform while migrating. There is no silver bullet answer, but generally the end goal is transformation and improvement. The following chart shows a typical progression in an outsourcing relationship. In general the goal in the first few months is to not break anything and to ensure progress is made. Then, over time, as the processes and procedures are more dialed in for both parties, optimization begins to occur. (Note: Some may choose to optimize while migrating, but that is a choice best analyzed on a case-by-case basis. It depends on the organizational capacity, the uniqueness of the situation, and the overall project goals.)

Figure 8

The following chart came to me from one of our IT outsourced partners. It hits the nail on the head. They called the dip in performance the "Valley of Implementation," and anyone who has been through a large IT systems implementation knows what this is like. Or if you have switched from a PC to a Mac you know that it feels awkward for the first few weeks or even months. But soon enough, you become even more efficient on the Mac than you ever were on the PC and your overall productivity is improved.

Figure 9

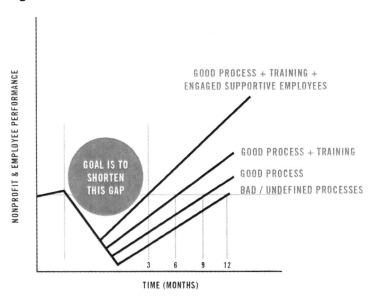

For organizations, the more you invest in improved processes, training, and ensuring you have engaged, supportive employees, the shorter the dip in productivity and the faster you will realize your return on investment from the time and energy spent in making the switch. So you don't have to get your house in order before you outsource, but you do want process improvements to be part of the plan.

Outsourcing is a very co-dependent partnership.

Secondly it is worth noting that outsourcing is a very co-dependent partnership. Outsourcing vendors rely on their clients for data, information, and compliance with processes. Nonprofits rely on their vendors to achieve certain service levels and to be trustworthy and reliable. When one fails, the other is hurt. Clients are dependent on the vendor for success, and vendors are reliant on the client to help them achieve that success.

For example, at Jitasa we are not physically located at a nonprofit's office. So when an invoice is received in the mail by the nonprofit, they need to open that letter, scan it, and send it to Jitasa. We have zero knowledge of that invoice arriving or when it is due. If the nonprofit fails to submit the invoice, the bill may not be paid on time, and Jitasa looks bad. So we are relying on the client to send us that information. Likewise, when the client properly submits that invoice to us, it gets assigned to that client's dedicated team, and if our team transposes the date and enters the payment date as August 7th instead of July 8th, the bill may also be paid late. Just as we are relying on the client, the client is relying on us.

As another example, at Jitasa we take care to prepare the executive director (ED) for the presentation of the organization's financials at board meetings. Board meetings are moments each month when it is vital that the accounting and reports are ready, otherwise the ED will look bad in front of the board. If Jitasa fails to prepare the reports on time, we both look bad. If the client fails to

> **Partners help redefine the processes and procedures of an organization and can help bring order to chaos.**

send us documentation in a timely fashion so that it is impossible to have the reports ready, we both look bad. We depend on the client and the client depends on us. We like to say we join our client's roster, so we are all part of the same team moving in the same direction.

Because of this co-dependent relationship, outsourcing partners naturally help create the need for process discipline. Partners help redefine the processes and procedures of an organization and can help bring order to chaos. At Jitasa, almost by definition, we help transform the processes and procedures of our clients from day one. To follow the example regarding the invoice, perhaps the organization did not have a form for coding invoices or classifying those invoices. So then we give them a template to use. From day one, we help them create improved processes and procedures to ensure that we can do our job.

That said, outsourced partners are somewhat limited in their ability to enforce process discipline. Nonprofits in internal disarray who view outsourcing as the silver bullet that can save them are highly likely to be disappointed. On the other hand, outsourced vendors should not require people to have their house in order when they arrive. Counselors don't require people to be perfect when they come in; people just need to show some willingness to change. It is the same with outsourcing relationships. It requires willingness to change, and a willingness to embrace new levels of process discipline. Nonprofits in internal disarray that are committed to improving may well find that an outsourced partner is just what they need to spark a change and to continually reinforce process discipline.

OWNERSHIP
CAN I OUTSOURCE EVERYTHING AND NOT HAVE TO WORRY ABOUT IT *AT ALL*?

It can be tempting for executive directors to want to abdicate responsibility when working with an outsourced provider. "Whew, not my problem any more!" It is important to note that although these are co-dependent relationships, ultimately the outcomes and performance of a nonprofit organization are the responsibility of the executive director / CEO. The buck stops with the executive director and the board.

Even though the nonprofit may not be doing the outsourced work, nonprofits are the owners of it. Executive directors may not know how to generate and produce all of the financial reports, but they do need to understand them and be able to report on them to the board. The same goes for outsourced HR, IT, or other aspects of the organization. You don't have to know how to write software code to manage an IT vendor, but you do need to know and understand what they are working on. At the end of the day, some knowledge is required to make the right decisions for the organization. Good vendors will help you in that process. They can explain what they are doing, explain why it is necessary, and give you the tools to make appropriate decisions. This is capacity building without giving up ownership.

If you are an executive director/CEO, CFO (chief financial officer), or COO (chief operating officer), this should give you relief. Outsourcing frees you from having to be good at one more thing. Rather than having to know it all, you just need to get really good at a few things—normally things you love to do as well.

This is capacity building without giving up ownership.

It is worth noting that vendor and contract management is an important skillset to have to effectively manage outsourcing relationships. Managing vendors can be quite different from managing employees. The nice thing is that it tends to take far less time to manage a vendor than an employee. From my experience, project management and effectively garnering resources are two key skills that most executive directors possess. They are accustomed to pulling together vendors, volunteers, board members, and other parties to achieve a common goal. Most executive directors are experienced at assembling teams—often virtually and ever-changing—to achieve goals. These same skills translate well into outsourced vendor management.

Lastly, as it relates to ownership, there are multiple delivery models that can be employed. You may choose to outsource an entire function—such as HR—or you may choose to only outsource a subset of that function—say, benefits management. You can blend together a mix of in-house staff and outsourced expertise to achieve a common purpose. Larger organizations may choose to go with a "best of breed" solution that incorporates multiple-outsourced partners. Others choose to single-outside source and partner with a single vendor to simplify management and improve integration. These choices are not overly complex for small organizations, but can be very complex for larger organizations. Outsourcing advisory firms exist, such as Equaterra at KPMG, to help organizations think through these decisions. For larger engagements—say involving contracts of $10 million-plus—a third party advisor is recommended. It is akin to hiring a marriage counselor to help during the dating and engagement period. Counseling services can help both sides move to a productive and healthy long-term relationship.

TOO EMBARRASSED TO ADMIT WHAT WE DON'T KNOW

One psychological barrier to outsourcing is admitting what we do not know. Many of us don't like to admit what we are not good at. It's embarrassing. **A common psychological trait is to cover up deficiencies with defensiveness. A friend of mine at the Nonprofit Finance Fund calls it the "persistence of ignorance."**

In general, I know we all believe that we don't need to be good at everything. I am perfectly happy admitting I have no idea how a car works. My wife is a mechanical engineer who worked in the body shop at General Motors. She's certainly more capable than me; she just doesn't have the interest or time to do it. Even if I had the time or interest, I'm not even quite sure which is the engine and which is the radiator. I couldn't reliably change the oil if my life depended on it. We both, for different reasons, happily outsource to our local mechanic. When our dishwasher began leaking all over the floor, it didn't even cross my mind to fix it myself. I called the dishwasher guy.

In our organizations, we need to have the same self-awareness of our strengths. We need to understand where we excel and where we need to get out of the way to allow others to excel. Nonprofit leaders who are thrust into leadership positions after a lifetime of running programs or doing hands-on social work may rightly feel intimidated by the incredible task of running a nonprofit. In November of 2011, Aaron Hurst, the President of the Taproot Foundation, wrote an article for the Huffington Post titled "It's Harder to Run a Nonprofit than a Company" (http://www.huffingtonpost.com/aaron-hurst/its-harder-to-run-a-nonpr_b_1095125.html). He lays out six very convincing arguments on why this is true. With this, on top of capacity-building consultants running around the country telling the world that there is a dearth of nonprofit leadership, it is no wonder nonprofit leaders may be a little gun-shy. The human reaction to all this negative press and pressure is to close up and work to prove, "Folks, we do know everything."

> A common psychological trait is to cover up deficiencies with defensiveness. A friend of mine at the Nonprofit Finance Fund calls it the "persistence of ignorance."

This is not necessarily the best reaction. Nonprofit leaders need the confidence to focus on what they do best, and happily admit to the areas where they need help or outside expertise. This will build capacity in our sector.

CLOSING

FOCUS ON YOUR CORE

At Jitasa, a firm dedicated to providing outsourced services for non-profits, we outsource many things. We outsource our IT, parts of the HR function, portions of our marketing, and much more. I want our team of bookkeepers and accountants singularly focused on our clients and their needs. I want them to excel at nonprofit accounting. The fewer distractions they have, the better. We are focused on engaging the nonprofit community and providing outstanding client service. Everything else is a distraction that we outsource.

Ask yourself, at the very core, what gives you and your organization energy? Where do you achieve the best results? What drains your energy? Where do you struggle? When you have developed that list, begin to prioritize where and how you can tackle these tasks. Perhaps it is simply through delegation to another staff member, or perhaps outsourcing is the answer. We have included a link at the back of this book which will take you to a simple assessment questionnaire. This is a good place to start your journey towards building capacity and strengthening your organization.

Outsourcing is an organizational strategy that, used effectively, can significantly improve the capacity within the nonprofit sector. Capacity building need not be focused on teaching individuals how to do everything. Capacity building needs to be focused on the organization as a whole and how to help achieve program outcomes with limited resources. By doing what you do best, you will feel energized as an individual and as an organization. Doesn't that sound appealing?

AFTERWORD

We have all read management books and attended seminars that discuss why some businesses prosper and some fail. The conversations tend to center around leadership qualities and why some leaders derail while others take their organizations to new heights. The experts will tell you that it's the strategic plan that really matters, while others will point to a laser-focus on a company's core competency.

I think I've probably seen virtually every word used to describe THE key component of success, but it has recently occurred to me that one word is missing from our lexicon. That word is courage. In the context of outsourcing, it is courage that is the single greatest determinant as to whether one will even examine such a possibility and, importantly, whether one will ultimately succeed in that endeavor.

I have had the opportunity to be a part of successful and not-so-successful outsourcing activities. As every consultant will tell you at the beginning of the process, it is of utmost importance that there is "leadership buy-in" around the effort. This not only means that the leadership (in the case of nonprofits this includes the senior leadership team and the Board of Directors) supports the initial examination and analysis about outsourcing certain functions but that they also are willing to, as William Shakespeare noted, take on the "slings and arrows of outrageous fortune".

Outsourcing is not easy and it is rarely, if ever, perfectly executed in its initial stages. It is, therefore, critically important that leadership sets the right tone and expectation at the beginning of the process. I often tell internal stakeholders that there is only one thing I could guarantee about the outsourcing process we were about to embark on and that was it would not go perfectly.

The infamous "80/20" rule needs to apply and everyone needs to understand that proposition. In fact, this is not such a bad thing. One learns from mistakes (often more than from successes) and a better process and end result ensues if people are willing to accept some bumpy roads. This, again, requires courage as the leadership will be at the tip of the arrow when it comes to explaining why thing didn't go exactly according to plan. Telling folks up front about how this change will occur may help to mitigate the arrows that will most assuredly come flying later on in the process.

Outsourcing also requires courage as, almost by definition, there is risk involved in moving away from "what we always do." I would submit that one of the nonprofit sector's greatest frailties is our inability to take appropriate risks and embrace the "not-so-perfect" outcome. It is perhaps more pronounced in our sector because we often have to have a more inclusive and collaborative process in any kind of major change. This collaborative approach is, again, actually a good thing as we get more buy-in up front than one might traditionally see in a for-profit environment.

Additionally, we might also increase the odds of getting the right answer as a result of that broad input. However, because of this nonprofit cultural phenomenon, we are less apt to be bold. It requires too much work to get everyone on board. We certainly won't achieve unanimity on anything we might want to do to move our organization forward. And, god forbid, if something doesn't go perfectly, we have the naysayers barking at our heels.

Thus, the organization and its leadership must have the courage to accept that some in the organization will never support the effort. These will be the people that will shout the loudest when the initial implementation doesn't go exactly as planned. They will say "well, I'm not the kind of person that says I told you so, but, I told you so!" It is the courageous leader and organization that stands up and reminds such individuals that the end result will, in fact, make the organization better. While this sounds easy, I am often amazed at how often this doesn't occur.

Now, there might be a fine line between courage and recklessness but I would submit that, for the most part, we are rarely making life and death decisions in an outsourcing activity. We certainly don't want to be reckless. We are running nonprofits where we often have people dependent on us to deliver on our services. I would suggest, however, that being risky sets a longer-term culture that will benefit the organization for years to come. It is a culture that embraces change, embraces innovation and embraces the notion that we can be perpetually better at what we do.

While some might argue, I don't believe our society sees the nonprofit sector as the hotbed of innovation and there is a reason for this. I believe we are often not willing to take on risks to better ourselves and our organizations. We are too concerned about what might happen if something goes wrong rather than wondering how things are already not going as well as they could because we don't innovate. It is the courageous leader and organization that is willing to move the culture of their organization to this outcome.

Outsourcing requires leaders to embrace this type of culture, and for the most part, this is a fairly new concept in the nonprofit community. Importantly, there are often direct financial benefits to such a move. Some of these are fairly straightforward as one can often quantify some kind of labor arbitrage by moving to an outsourced environment. It is normally the case, although not always, that having individual units of a nonprofit doing certain back office functions (i.e., finance) is less cost-effective than centralizing that activity in one location. This is simply a result of what we all learned in economics 101 related to economies of scale.

Perhaps as important, there are also qualitative advantages to moving to such an environment. For example, moving certain back-office operations to an outsourced environment mitigates issues that arise with staff turnover. This is especially true for smaller nonprofits. When your finance person leaves, you are in an immediate crisis as that skillset may not be nascent in another staff member. Thus, you go along for months without producing financial reports to your Board or a Board member has to step in to take on those responsibilities. This should not occur.

In an outsourced environment, the company doing your back-office work has a host of individuals that can "pick up the slack" and these folks already have the skills to jump right in and handle the client's activities. I can point to examples of small nonprofits who rail against the idea of moving to an outsourced environment. Yet, these same entities have ended up paying more in overage fees to their external auditors than they would have paid for a full year's worth of services from an outsourcing firm because the auditors had to spend additional hours cleaning up and testing the inadequate financial activities of the entity. In this true-life example, I would submit that it takes more courage to "let go" than to keep trying to carry out these activities in-house.

It is clear to me that it is not very hard to keep doing what you are doing. It doesn't take any courage. It does, however, take courage to give up some level of control of your back office activities. Interestingly, what I find is that, for the most part, one is really not giving up much control at all when moving to an outsourced environment. You are still in charge of your data. You are still in control of your transactions. Your vendors will be paid. Your Board will get monthly financial statements. In fact, those statements might be better and more accurate than ever before! The outsourcing firm is simply providing a service.

Moving your organization's culture to one that is open to outsourcing requires an emotional, not an intellectual change in mindset. One could point to analytics that would show that it is more cost-effective to outsource certain functions. Intellectually, we can all get that. Yet, people will steadfastly refuse to even discuss the notion because of the emotional need to "be in control." It takes courage to give up that need for control.

This book has put forth the proposition that nonprofits should focus on what we do best. It, thus, suggests that there may be some things we do that others can do better. It might actually make sense to give up some of our work so that the "comparative advantage" can take its full course. We do what we do best and let others do what we don't do so well!

I have always assumed that most of us work in the nonprofit environment to "do good work." While some have certainly joined our organizations to oversee human resources, IT and financial activities, for most of us we came into this sector to make a difference in someone else's life, to make the world a little bit better. I have rarely met a nonprofit CEO who couldn't wait to get into the office to do payroll! No. They wanted to come into the office to fundraise or carry out some amazing program. But in order to focus on what they do best, they must be willing to entertain the possibility that their organization would be better if they let someone else do some things for them. But that takes courage.

Kurt Kroemer
COO, Humanity United
Former COO, Make-A-Wish Foundation

APPENDIX

WHAT NOW?

Take 15 minutes to answer these quick questions. Or, hop online at www.jitasa.is/best-book-survey to complete this online. Do it yourself and send to others on your staff, your board, key volunteers, or key donors. The online questionnaire will email results to you and anyone else you choose.

1. What are your organization's core competencies? What do you do better than other similar organizations? What makes your organization unique?

2. What gives your team members energy? What drains your team? What does your team do well? What does your team do not-so-well?

3. What are your personal strengths and weaknesses? What gives you energy? What drains you and de-motivates you?

4. Fill in Figure 10, by writing these functions into the 2x2 matrix:
   a. Programs (feel free to list out each of your programs)
   b. Fundraising—Marketing & Publications
   c. Fundraising—Donor data management
   d. Fundraising—Grants
   e. Fundraising—Events
   f. Administrative HR functions
   g. IT infrastructure
   h. IT applications
   i. Website management
   j. Bookkeeping & Accounting
   k. Payroll
   l. Budgeting
   m. Other business processes . . .

For smaller organizations, <10 employees, the vertical axis will relate to the executive director's personal feelings on time. What gives her energy? What does she enjoy doing?

For larger organizations, or nationally federated nonprofits, the vertical axis relates more to core competencies and future organizational focus. Where does the leadership want people to focus their time and energy? What is the profile of your typical leaders in the organization—do you attract passionate program people, or administrative types? When looking over your network and the people attracted to your organization, can you make some assumptions regarding their skills and their preferences around the use of their time?

Figure 10

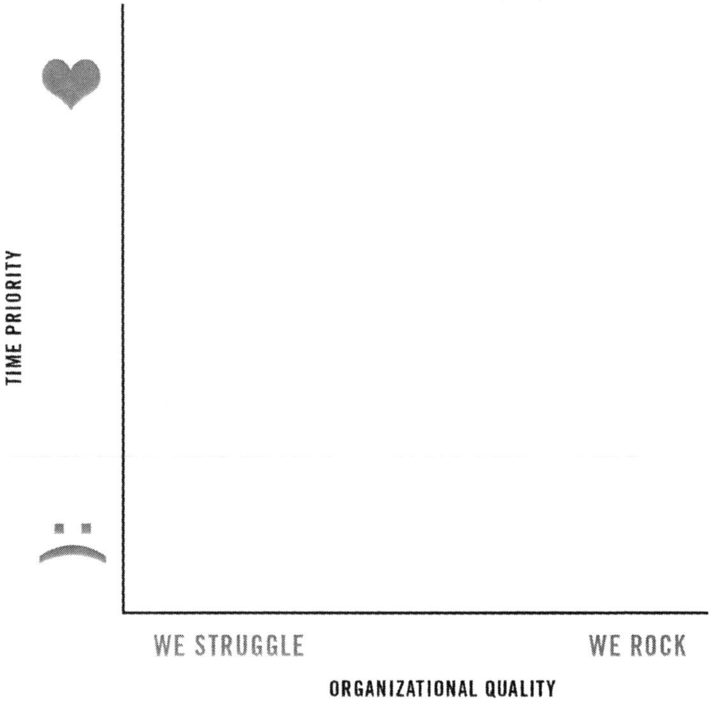

TIME PRIORITY

WE STRUGGLE   WE ROCK

ORGANIZATIONAL QUALITY

Now compare your answers for Figure 10 with Figure 11.

Figure 11

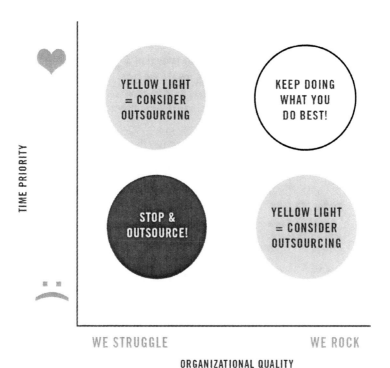

5. Cost is also a consideration when considering outsourcing. For the areas you put into the red zone or the yellow zone, estimate the following: *(This question may require a little homework or a small project to determine the existing costs and the costs of an outsourcing provider or two.)*

a. Current direct cost per year: $_____

b. Current indirect cost per year: $_____

c. Cost with an outsourcing provider: $_____

d. Outsourcing will: (circle one)

    i. Save us money

    ii. Be cost-neutral

    iii. Be more expensive, but worth it because of the time savings and / or increase in quality

    iv. Be too expensive, can't justify making the change

Once you have gone through this simple exercise, you can begin to build an organizational roadmap that will help you determine the best use of your scarce resources (time and money). Perhaps you start by outsourcing one function that falls into the red quadrant. Once this is successful, tackle another area. Or if you like all of your change at once and have buy-in from key staff, consider outsourcing multiple functions.

This simple checklist should allow you to structure your thoughts and structure the conversation regarding the best way to build or reorganize your organization. And ultimately, it should help you focus on doing what you do best.

CREATE COMMON GOOD

Create Common Good receives proceeds from the sale of this book.

Create Common Good uses food to change lives.

Mission:

We provide training and employment to refugees and others in need. Our experiential programs transform lives by teaching others to fish and by bringing access to fresh, conveniently prepared, local food products.

Why Create Common Good?

A self-sufficient and healthy population is more than a quality of life indicator: it's an economic investment. By serving refugee and low-income families through our training, employment and healthy food access programs, we're creating opportunities to address unemployment, public service dependency, rising medical care costs and obesity.

How?

- Training: by providing job training and employment in food-related industries, we can help individuals attain self-sufficiency. In the last four years, we have trained more than 300 adult refugee head of households, putting $6 million of earned wages back into the Idaho economy.
- Feeding: 13.5% of Idahoans receive food assistance from food pantries. 77% of adults and 81% of children in Idaho

do not eat the recommended number of servings of fruits and vegetables. CCG is working in community collaborations to address this by increasing access to fresh, healthy, prepared foods, providing low-income families the nutrition they need but often cannot access.

www.createcommongood.org

NO TREES WERE HARMED
IN THE MAKING OF THIS BOOK

OK, so a few
did need to make the ultimate sacrifice.

In order to steward our environment,
we are partnering with *Plant With Purpose*, to plant
a tree for every tree that paid the price for the printing of
this book.

ABOUT JITASA

Jitasa, formerly Easy Office, is a social venture providing affordable finance and accounting services for 200+ nonprofits nationwide. Jitasa was founded in 2007 by a group of Yale MBAs and The Momentum Group, now known as Create Common Good, a 501c3 organization. Jitasa exists solely to serve the needs of nonprofits and is a certified B Corporation.

www.Jitasa.is

ABOUT THE AUTHOR

Jeff Russell is the Founder and CEO of Jitasa. Prior to Jitasa, Jeff had over a decade of consulting, client management and back-office experience working for Accenture and PACCESS, a mid-sized international supply chain company. He served as the Executive Director for an international development nonprofit, The Momentum Group. As an industrial engineer, Jeff is passionate about helping nonprofits become more effective and efficient. Jeff is a Georgia Tech Industrial Engineer and holds an MBA from Yale University.

And most importantly, Jeff is the proud father of two beautiful children and one beautiful wife. Jeff's family lives in beautiful Boise, Idaho where they enjoy biking, skiing, running, and the finest potatoes in all the world.